A Black Hole Is NOT a Hole

Are you sure about that?

A Black Hole Is NOT a Hole

Carolyn Cinami DeCristofano

Illustrated by **Michael Carroll**

Charlesbridge

To Alyssa Mito Pusey, who heard a book's worth of possibility in a short conversation. Working with you is one of my greatest professional joys and privileges.

I would also like to express my deep respect and appreciation to Judy O'Malley. Her experience, vision, and vitality helped shape this book.—C. C. D.

To Caroline, Andrew, and Alexandra, the stars in my life; and to my cars, the financial black holes of my universe.—M. C.

Published by Charlesbridge
85 Main Street
Watertown, MA 02472
(617) 926-0329
www.charlesbridge.com

Library of Congress Cataloging-in-Publication Data
DeCristofano, Carolyn Cinami.
    A black hole is not a hole / Carolyn Cinami DeCristofano;
Illustrated by Michael Carroll.
        p. cm.
    Includes index.
    ISBN 978-1-57091-783-7 (reinforced for library use)
1. Black holes (Astronomy)—Juvenile literature. I. Carroll, Michael,
ill. II. Title.
QB843.B55D43 2011
523.8'875—dc22   2010022764

Printed in China
(hc) 10 9 8 7 6 5 4 3 2 1

Illustrations done in acrylics and Adobe Photoshop
Type set in Palatino, Palatino Informal Sans, and Blambot
Color separations by KHL Chroma Graphics, Singapore
Printed and bound September 2011 by Jade Productions
    in Heyuan, Guangdong, China
Production supervision by Brian G. Walker
Designed by Susan Mallory Sherman

Title page:
Black holes inspire both scientists and artists. This illustration of a black hole and its surroundings is based on what scientists understand about black holes.

Table of Contents

Introduction

Have you heard the news?

In outer space, mysterious entities called black holes seem up to no good.

From the headlines, you'd think black holes were beasts with endless appetites, lying in wait for the next meal. By some reports they are "runaway," out-of-control "predators" that "feed" on galaxies, only to "belch" and "spit out" what they don't eat. They "lurk" in the shadows, "mangling" stars and "gobbling" them up. In short, they have a nasty reputation for being monsters "gone mad."

But you know what?

A black hole isn't a monster. It's not even alive. That means it can't lurk, eat, or belch. It has no dark, destructive desires.

Of course, you may have already figured this out. But you know what else?

A black hole is NOT a hole—
at least not the kind you can
dig in the ground
or poke your finger through.
You can't just walk along
and fall into one.
A black hole isn't a hole
like that.

If a black hole is not a hole,
then what in the universe is it?

Places with Pull

A black hole is a place in space with a powerful pull.

Way out beyond where you are right now, beyond the clouds, beyond the Moon, beyond Pluto, beyond our solar system, space goes on and on. You could travel for trillions of miles and you'd barely get to the closest star. In another few trillion miles you might pass another star. Space is that huge.

Way out there, trillions, quadrillions, and even more *-illions* of miles away, are special places called black holes. These places in space are special because of their powerful pull on other things. A black hole's pull is the strongest pull in the entire universe.

Nothing can out-tug a black hole. No army of tow trucks, no convoy of supersized earth haulers, no fleet of giant rocket engines. Not all of them combined.

A black hole pulls in nearby dust. It pulls in nearby asteroids. It pulls in nearby stars and even nearby starlight. And no light, stars, asteroids, or dust comes out. Not ever.

The super-pulling power of a black hole is enough to haul in entire stars. In this artist's image, a black hole reels in glowing gas from a nearby star. (The star itself is out of the picture frame.)

How Far Out Is Way Out There?

Black holes are way out beyond where you are right now—much farther away than the edge of our solar system. To talk about the distance to a black hole, you'd need a huge number.

How huge? Well, in your everyday life, you probably travel only a few miles (or kilometers). At most, you might go tens of miles. Longer trips might be in the hundreds or even thousands of miles. In outer space, these distances would seem smaller than baby steps. Out there, you'd need to stock up on zeroes to describe how far it is from one place to another.

From Earth to the Sun: *millions* of miles or kilometers

From the Sun to the next closest star: *tens of trillions* of miles or kilometers

From Earth to the nearest black hole: *quadrillions* of miles or kilometers

Distance across our galaxy (Milky Way): *hundreds of quadrillions* of miles or kilometers

Distance across the observable universe (which may be much smaller than the whole universe): *sextillions* of miles or kilometers

Hundred	100
Thousand	1,000
Million	1,000,000
Billion	1,000,000,000
Trillion	1,000,000,000,000
Quadrillion	1,000,000,000,000,000
Quintillion	1,000,000,000,000,000,000
Sextillion	1,000,000,000,000,000,000,000
Septillion	1,000,000,000,000,000,000,000,000
Octillion	1,000,000,000,000,000,000,000,000,000
Nonillion	1,000,000,000,000,000,000,000,000,000,000

In the universe, enormous distances separate even "close" neighbors. The Sun and Pluto, for instance, are a staggering 3,647,240,000 miles (5,869,660,000 kilometers) apart—yet that's just a hop, skip, and jump, astronomically speaking! (Sizes and distances in this diagram are not to scale.)

Sun

Mercury

Venus

Earth and its Moon

Mars

A black hole is like a giant whirlpool.

Have you ever pulled out a sink stopper and watched water swirl down the drain? Spirals of water flow toward the center. You've made a small whirlpool.

Imagine a bigger whirlpool in a river. Far away, nobody knows it's there. Boats chug and sail along. Schools of fish dart by, following their fishy urges. Closer to the whirlpool, it's a different story.

A fish swimming near the whirlpool's edge feels a gentle tug as the current drags it toward the spinning center. No problem. With a little swish, the fish can speed up, giving itself the oomph to swim away. After putting some distance between itself and the whirlpool, the fish no longer feels the current's inward pull.

But what if the fish drifted farther in?

Closer to the center of the whirlpool, the pull would grow stronger. To escape the whirlpool, the fish would have to swim faster than it had to at the edge. Even closer to the middle, if the fish couldn't go much faster, it would find itself swept all the way in, stuck in the swirl, pulled round and round and round.

A black hole works something like that whirlpool.

Even though a black hole's pull is the strongest in the universe, it's not strong from far away. Galaxies and stardust drifting through space don't get dragged into a distant black hole.

However, near a black hole, gases and dust and stars encounter its tug. Some things may be hurtling by so fast they won't get pulled into the black hole. Other things may not be as swift. They will be drawn in.

Closer and closer, the tugging force gets stronger and stronger. Close enough, the black hole no longer acts like a whirlpool.

What a drag!

The inward pull of a swirling whirlpool gets stronger near its center. The closer a fish (or anything else) gets to the center, the more speed it needs to get out.

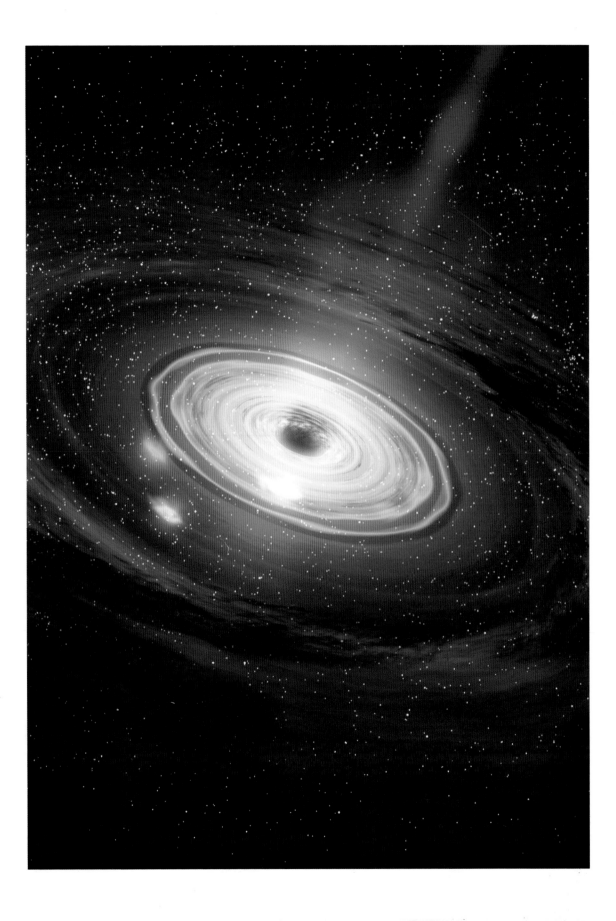

Even though it's like a whirlpool, a black hole is not a whirlpool.

With a whirlpool, there's always a fast-enough fish—or a fast-enough *something*—that moves so quickly it won't be pulled all the way into the center.

Not so with a black hole! Within a certain distance the black hole's power is so strong, nothing is fast enough to zip away.

This is a black hole's special trait: its super-pulling zone. Outside the zone, there's always the chance that something will zoom past and away. But anything inside this zone stays in the black hole's place in space forever. Nothing else in the universe is so inescapable.

So a black hole is NOT a whirlpool. It just (sort of) acts like one.

There's another difference. In a whirlpool, the swirling current of water draws the fish into the center. But a black hole isn't made of water. Something else drives its pulling power.

Like a fish caught in a whirlpool, colorful, glowing gases swirl toward a black hole. The dark center marks the black hole's super-pulling zone. (Artist's representation)

The Pulling Power of a Black Hole

A black hole is an extreme gravity zone.

Gravity is the source of a black hole's super pull.

You deal with gravity every day. You count on it to bring you back to the ground when you jump up. You depend on it when you try to catch a pop fly, knowing the ball will fall down. You expect it to be there, even if you don't think about it much.

People must have always noticed that objects fall, but they didn't know what made this happen. They certainly didn't guess that falling objects had anything to do with the stars, Moon, planets, and Sun—but then one man came along with some new ideas.

Gravity Rules

Just outside a black hole's extreme gravity zone, its gravitation is still remarkable. In this artist's picture, a black hole pulls clouds of gas off a nearby star.

That man was Isaac Newton. In 1687 he proposed that objects fall to the ground because Earth pulls on them. But his idea reached beyond Earth. He suggested that *all* things pull on each other, even when they are not touching. He considered this pull a force of nature and referred to it as *gravitas*—what we now call gravity.

What a wise guy.

According to Newton, the force of gravity is a two-way tug between any two objects. It works with anything—any matter at all. The matter can be a tiny bit of a thing, as small as a speck of stardust. It can be a huge collection of material, as gigantic as a galaxy. It can be as rigid as rock or as flimsy as flame. No matter what it is, if it's made of matter, then it possesses the power to pull on anything else.

Newton also noted that in any situation, the strength of the pull depends on how much matter, or mass, is involved. When there's a lot of matter, there's a strong pull. Less matter means a weaker pull. For example, imagine a fluffy snowball and a harder-packed snowball of the same size. The fluffier ball is made of less stuff. Its pull is wimpier than the pull of the densely packed ball.

You can feel this difference when you hold the two snowballs in your hands. Each one presses down on your hand because of the gravitational attraction it shares with Earth. The hard-packed snowball has a stronger attraction to Earth because it is made of more material. It presses more forcefully than the fluffy one. It feels heavier.

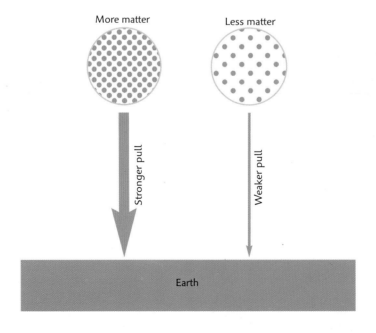

Gravity works everywhere in the universe (as far as anyone can tell). It's gravity that holds the solar system together. Even faraway Pluto and Neptune, as well as the outer comets, are gravitationally connected to the Sun. Instead of flying off into other parts of space, they stay in our solar neighborhood. The Sun's gravitational pull extends so far out because the Sun has a lot of matter packed into it—about five hundred times the mass of everything else in the solar system combined!

Even so, our Sun and solar system are just a tiny part of the universe. Most things are too far away to be swept in by the Sun's gravity. Thanks again to Newton, we know that the closer things are, the harder they pull on each other, and the farther apart they are, the weaker they pull.

Closer objects have a stronger pull

Farther objects have a weaker pull

This is true for all matter in the universe, including black holes. It's just that with black holes, the close-up effect is extreme.

Facts of the Matter

How densely packed is the material that forms a black hole? Imagine a black hole the size of a snowball. Now compare it to a "snowball" made of different materials.

A snowball-sized	Has a mass of	This weighs about the same as
Ball of fluffy snow	37 grams	A slice of bread
Ball of hard-packed snow	87 grams	A small candy bar
Rock (granite)	287 grams	A rock, of course!
Ball of plasma from the Sun's center	29,000 grams	An 8- or 9-year-old human
Black hole[‡]	50 octillion grams	10 Earths

[‡]In a black hole the size of a snowball, most of the "snowball" would be empty space (the extreme gravity zone) surrounding a densely packed center. The center would contain all the mass, yet take up less room than a single snowflake.

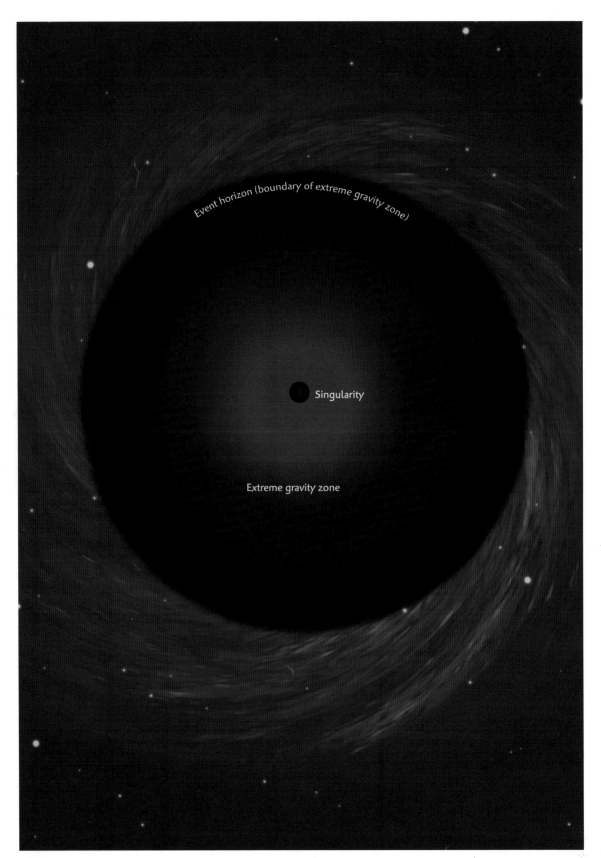

An Extreme Case of Gravity

Remember that super-pulling space around a black hole—the one with the strongest pull in the universe? That super pull is the close-up gravitational power of a black hole. Here in this zone, the gravity is so intense that nothing can move fast enough to fly, launch, jump, or zoom away.

Around this extreme zone is a boundary called the event horizon. This boundary acts like a point of no return. Once past it, there's no going back. Only black holes have such extreme gravity zones, and only black holes have event horizons. This is what makes a black hole different from everything else.

But a black hole is more than just a gravity zone—more than just empty space inside an event horizon. A black hole also includes the source of its tremendous gravitation: a massive amount of densely packed matter sitting at its center. The matter is so densely packed that it forms a single point, called a singularity.

Where does this matter come from? How did it get to be so densely packed? And what does it have to do with the beginning of a black hole?

The answers lie in the stars.

This cross-section diagram shows the anatomy of a black hole. At the center is an extremely small, densely packed singularity, super-enlarged for visibility. Surrounding the singularity is an extreme gravity zone, colored red. The outer boundary of this zone is the event horizon. (Diagram not to scale)

An Event What?

Have you ever watched the Sun set? After it sinks below the horizon, Earth blocks your view of it. Even though you know it's still out there in space, you can't see it. Any and all events on the Sun remain invisible to you for as long as it is below the horizon. If the Sun suddenly turned purple, you wouldn't see it happen.

In a similar way, once an object enters the extreme gravity zone of a black hole, the object disappears from view. Even though nothing physically blocks our sight, once the object is beyond the boundary of the zone, we cannot see what happens to it. Events beyond the black hole's "horizon" are invisible to us. Because of this visual effect, scientists named the boundary the *event horizon*.

What happens below the horizon stays below the horizon.

3

Black-Hole Beginnings

The beginning of a black hole can be the end of something else.

Black holes come from stars.

Every star has a beginning, when light first bursts from it. Then it shines on and on, for millions, even billions, of years. But every star comes to an end. And sometimes a star's final moments are an all-out frenzy. After the dust clears, a black hole may be all that's left.

Black hole's First picture

Awww . . .

Ignition! Scientists keep their eyes on this bright, active spot in the sky, where they can witness new star formation. Eventually the brilliance of some stars may give way to the darkness of a black hole. (False-color telescope image)

19

Star Power

Before a star is a star, it is an enormous cloud of gases. At the start, wisps of gas and drifts of dust collect, their gravity drawing them together. As more stuff gathers, its combined gravitation grows stronger. Eventually the cloud pulls itself into a massive ball of material.

Under the force of its own weight, the gigantic ball presses inward. Deep beneath the surface, the intense pressure squeezes the material, like the powerful grip of a giant hand. The inner material packs together tightly. More matter mounts up on the outside, increasing the pressure on the inside. Soon the pressure in the center is so high, it ignites a booming nuclear reaction. Starlight bursts from the ball of gas. Now blazing, flaring, spewing, and spouting, the new star is a fiery furnace.

Sparking a Star

A star's fiery nuclear reaction is not really a fire. Instead it is a dramatic melding, or blending, of atoms, called nuclear fusion.

Each atom has its own tiny center, or nucleus. Surrounding each nucleus is an electrical force field. Ordinarily, this force field repels other nuclei, pushing them away—but in a star, the nuclei meld. How come?

As the star material gathers, its inward pressure grows. The nuclei respond by zipping and zooming faster and faster, veering away from each other all the while. However, when the pressure gets high enough, the nuclei are going so fast that their speed overpowers their repulsion. Slamming into one another, they push through each other's force fields and fuse. As the nuclei meld, a smidgen of their matter vaporizes into energy. This creates a tremendous burst of furious noise, motion, and another by-product: star shine!

Like other stars, the Sun is a blazing ball of activity. As the brightest and hottest material rolls and swirls, darker, less-hot material sinks toward the center. The flare in the upper right is a tremendous whip of plasma lashing out into space. (False-color telescope image)

In the star's center, the gas is so energized that it has become a sort of super gas, called plasma. The hot plasma is in constant motion. It expands like hot air inside a balloon and pushes outward from the center. Meanwhile, the crushing weight of the star material continues to press inward. In goes the outer material and out goes the inner. The plasma rolls and churns like a hyper hurricane of heat, light, sound, and motion.

The star ball holds together in this perfectly balanced commotion for millions or billions of years, until the star's nuclear furnace runs out of fuel. The reaction suddenly ceases.

When that happens—look out! The end of the star is near.

Out of Fuel, Out of Time

This is a blast!

Some stars go out in a blaze of glory.

Once the nuclear reactions stop, the star's center begins to cool. The plasma slows down, its outward push growing weak. The balance is broken. The plasma collapses in on itself.

In one giant, sudden *WHOOOOOSH!*, the center of the star compresses. It caves in, growing denser and tighter than ever.

CRASH! This core material bumps—hard!—against itself.

BOOM! The material rebounds like an ocean wave slamming against a rock cliff. It pushes on the star's outer gases, which flow outward in giant surges of heat and light. As the star material rushes outward, the star grows and grows until it is a supernova, or super star. What happens next?

Possibly a black hole forms. Possibly not.

In this artist's illustration, a massive star comes to a spectacular end, its gases rebounding from the dense center and surging outward in bursts of light, heat, and motion.

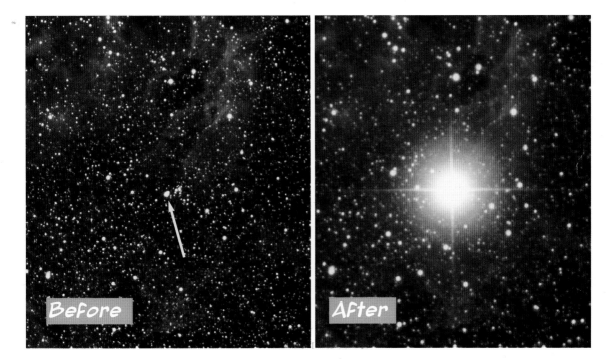

Before

After

In 1987 a distant star appeared as a pinpoint in the "before" picture before bursting out as the brilliant supernova in the "after" shot.

It all depends on the original mass of the star. If the star was about twenty-five to forty times the size of our Sun, then what's left of the star's center goes into a sudden collapse, called fallback. Once again, the star stuff plunges inward under its own weight. In, in, in it pulls. Tighter and tighter the material contracts, crunching in so fast and so hard that it is destroyed. Even its atoms are utterly demolished.

All the matter that once filled the center of the star shrinks down to a single, tiny point of extremely dense mass. It has no recognizable parts. But it does have one feature that makes it unique.

It has a pull of gravity so strong that it can out-pull anything else in the universe. Nothing can out-tug it. No army of tow trucks, no convoy of supersized earth haulers, no fleet of giant rocket engines. Not all of them combined.

Do you recognize this pull? It's the pull of a black hole. The star, a big, brilliant ball of light, has turned into a dark place of enormous gravitation. A black hole has formed.

What Happens to the Other Stars?

All stars run out of fuel, but not all stars end up as black holes. Which stars form what?

If the star is up to nine times the mass of the Sun:

Such a low-mass star never becomes a supernova. Instead, its inner core turns into a small, whitish ball of cooling material called a white dwarf. Every day you see a lightweight star that is destined to become a white dwarf: the Sun!

(Artist's representation)

If the star is nine to twenty-five times the mass of the Sun:

The star is not quite heavy enough to form a black hole. It goes through a supernova, but when it falls back on itself, its gravity isn't strong enough to crunch the material into a singularity. Instead, it forms another type of star, called a neutron star. Like other stars, neutron stars are ball-shaped and emit light, but they are much denser. Only black holes have a greater density.

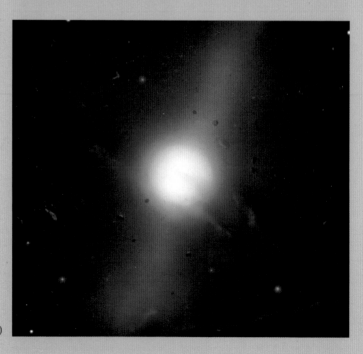

(Artist's representation)

If the star is twenty-five to forty times the mass of the Sun:

The gases blast out as the star goes supernova. Then the remaining material collapses inward, forming a black hole by fallback (see page 23).

(Artist's representation)

If the star is over forty times the mass of the Sun:

When this type of ultra-massive star runs out of fuel, it goes through an initial *WHOOOOOSH!* of collapse. However, because its enormous mass generates such tremendous gravitation, there's no *CRASH!* of a rebound or *BOOM!* that blasts gases out into a supernova. Instead, the matter just keeps on whooshing inward, directly forming a black hole.

(Artist's representation)

The Blackness of Black Holes

A black hole is black because no light comes from it.

A black hole is nothing to look at. Literally. If you could somehow take a close-up picture of a black hole, it wouldn't be one for the scrapbook. It would just be blank . . . and black.

The blackness of black holes is peculiar: although there's plenty of light within a black hole, you can't see it from the outside. Yet there's no wall physically blocking the light or bouncing it back in. Instead, gravity keeps the light contained.

Black hole all grown up!

This artist's illustration helps us imagine the utter darkness of a black hole, from which no light escapes.

Moving Light: The Movie

Pass the imaginary popcorn, please!

You may not think about it much, but light moves. It travels from one place to another, and that takes time.

But not much time. When light travels, it moves fast! Our eyes and brains can't keep up. But you *can* slow down light to see what's going on—if you run what's called a thought experiment. In a thought experiment, you use your imagination to conjure up an experiment you couldn't do in real life (at least not easily). Then you run things through in your mind and see what might happen. For this thought experiment, you'll need to imagine a slow-motion movie of light. (It's okay to imagine the popcorn, too.)

It's a misty night. In the darkness, a pinpoint of light becomes visible. Someone has turned on a flashlight. The pinpoint grows to the size of the bulb. Because this is slow motion, only the bulb is bright. Nothing else lights up—yet.

Now the light begins to spread outward from the bulb. It fills a bigger and bigger space. As the light moves forward, it strikes little fog droplets, the ground, a sneaker, a tree, a cat. After each collision, some light bounces off. It is redirected. Some of it reaches a person's eyes.

Only then can the light trigger the person's eyes and brain. In slow, stretched-out speech, the person says, "Loooooo-ooooook! Aaaaaaaaaaaa caaaaaa-aaat!"

With the action slowed down, you are able to notice the time it takes for the light to move outward from the bulb to the person's eyes. This was a short trip for the light. There wasn't much going on. On longer trips, more might happen. The light might encounter places of extra-intense gravity. Then things would get more interesting. Time for a sequel! This time, the action is set in outer space.

Measuring Distances with Light

How fast can you run in a second? Six feet? A couple of meters? In that same second, light would travel more than 900 million feet (about 300 million meters). That's almost from Earth to the Moon! This length can be called a light second because it is the distance light travels in a second. (A "kid second" would be those six feet you just sprinted.)

A light second might seem like a big distance, but compared to the universe, it's puny. Astronomers need much bigger units of length to describe the stretches of space between stars. One unit they use is the light year, which is the distance that light can travel through space in a single year.

A light year is about 31 quadrillion feet, or about 6 trillion miles (over 9.5 trillion kilometers). Compare this to a "kid year"—about 26 thousand miles (or a little under 42,000 kilometers)—though so far no kid has reported sprinting nonstop for an entire year!

The Sequel: Bending Light

In *Moving Light 2,* light is on the go again, this time in a slow-motion trek through the universe. You track its path as it moves outward from a star (instead of a flashlight). Some of it bounces off asteroids, gases, and dust in its way, just as it reflected off the droplets of fog on Earth.

However, as the light passes extra-massive objects—big stars, huge planets, whole galaxies—something else happens. The light changes direction. Pulled by the objects' gravity, it veers off its straight-line course. The more intense the gravity, the more the light's path bends.

Just outside the event horizon of a black hole, light's energy keeps it zipping along, like that fish swimming along the outer edge of a whirlpool. Although the black hole's gravity changes the light's path, the light doesn't swerve into the black hole.

However, if light *does* cross the event horizon, the greater intensity of gravity makes the light curve inward. As the light continues traveling in its new direction, it gets even closer to the center of the black hole, where gravity is even stronger. The closer the light gets to the center, the more gravity redirects it inward.

In this way, the light traces an inward spiral. Because the light never turns out again, it can't reach our eyes or a telescope. This utter absence of outward-bound light is why a black hole is black.

From the outside, a black hole is invisible. But if it's invisible, then how can we know it's there? How can we find it—especially if it's quadrillions or more miles away?

Bending Starlight? What's the Evidence?

Can gravity really change the path of light? In 1919 the scientist Arthur S. Eddington led a team to investigate this question.

The team photographed the same stars at different times: once during the night and once during the day, when the starlight passed very close by the Sun on its way to Earth.[‡] If gravity *could* affect light, the Sun's powerful gravitation would "bend" the starlight, changing its path. This change would create the illusion that during the day the stars moved slightly from their nighttime positions.

After carefully comparing the photos, the scientists announced their results: the stars seemed to have moved! This was the first evidence that gravity does, in fact, affect light.

[‡]During the day, the Sun's bright light usually washes out background starlight. To photograph the daytime stars, Eddington's team worked during a solar eclipse, when the Moon blocks the Sun's light.

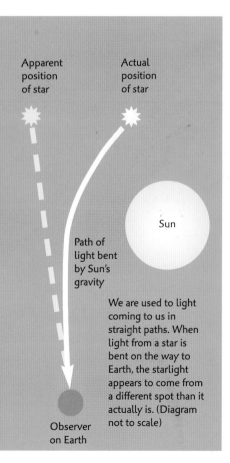

Apparent position of star

Actual position of star

Sun

Path of light bent by Sun's gravity

We are used to light coming to us in straight paths. When light from a star is bent on the way to Earth, the starlight appears to come from a different spot than it actually is. (Diagram not to scale)

Observer on Earth

Mission Impossible?
Seeking the Invisible

A black hole is like a hiding place in space, with footprints leading to it.

There's more to invisibility than what doesn't meet the eye. All sorts of things are invisible to us, for different reasons. Some, like atoms, are too tiny to see. Others, like a black cat on a dark night, aren't lit brightly enough.

Certain things are invisible to us because our eyes just can't sense them. You don't see beams of infrared light shooting across the room from your remote control to the TV, for example, or radio waves streaming off everyone's cell phone.

Then there's the invisibility caused by a black hole. No matter how hard you look, you can't see the black hole itself. There's nothing at all coming from it—no light, no other forms of energy, and no matter. We can detect only what's around it—never anything inside.

But there *are* clues that hint at the presence of black holes. Scientists use these clues to track them, the way you can follow footprints right up to someone's hiding place.

Thanks to telescopes that translate invisible energy into color-coded pictures, we can "see" red jets of invisible radio energy fountaining from the area of a black hole.

Outta sight!

On the Trail

One of the best black-hole clues is X-ray energy. As matter approaches an event horizon, its atoms "shine" with invisible X-rays. Although our eyes can't see the X-rays, we can make detectors that respond to their tremendous energy.

X-ray-catching telescopes make pictures of otherwise invisible X-rays. The pictures reveal that certain areas in outer space are emitting intense X-rays. Each bright location points out where something extraordinary is going on. It is a hint that a black hole might be there.

Acting on the hint, scientists search the X-rays for patterns that most likely signal black holes. One pattern is an X-ray ring that seems to surround nothing. The nothing part might be a black hole. If so, the ring is energy released by super-heated matter spiraling just outside the event horizon.

X-ray rings in space can clue scientists in to a possible black hole. (Artist's representation)

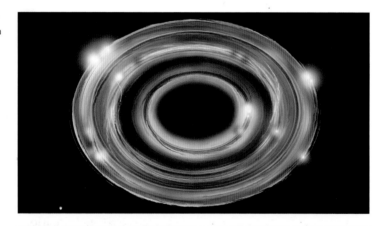

A Science Friction Story

X-rays can mark the spot of a black hole, but what generates them? Some exotic black-hole feature? Nope. The X-rays are generated by plain old friction. Friction is what makes your hands warm up when you rub them together really fast, or what makes rubber burn when a car screeches to a halt, tires skidding on the road. In the same way, material swirling in toward a black hole skids past other matter and heats up. As you might expect, near a black hole, the friction is extreme. The material heats up so much that it begins to glow—in invisible, super-powerful X-rays.

Scientists also seek patterns in the intensity of the X-rays. Just as you rely on the rise and fall of a melody's tune and volume to recognize a particular song, scientists look for a unique pattern in the rise and fall of the X-rays to identify a black hole.

Telltale signs of strong gravity may also point to a black hole. One spectacular gravity footprint appears as smudged, multiple images of galaxies. Such images can form when light from faraway galaxies passes near a black hole but does not cross the event horizon. Sometimes the galactic light splits up and bends around the black hole. Some light goes left and some goes right. Some goes up; some goes down. The beams of split-up light make it around the black hole but may not come back together again. Like reflections in a kaleidoscope, they create multiple images of the galaxy around the black hole.

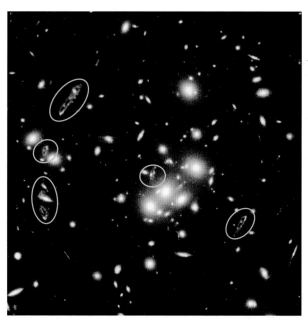

The circled blue smears in this picture are multiple images of just one distant galaxy. On its way to the telescope, the light from this galaxy passed a group of other galaxies. Their combined gravitation was strong enough to split the "blue" galaxy's light. A black hole can create the same kind of special effect, called gravitational lensing.

A star's motion can also reveal a black hole. Imagine two ice skaters gripping hands and whirling around each other. What if one of the skaters were somehow invisible? His partner's whirling motion would give him away. Similarly, if a visible star whirls around a dark area in space, its movement suggests an invisible partner. The more intense the gravity of the invisible partner, the faster the visible star will swing around it. If the visible star cuts a fast enough orbit, then chances are good that only the strongest of gravity sources—a black hole—is there.

One telltale sign of a black hole is the incredible speed at which a visible star whips around its invisible companion. The star GRO J1655-40, shown in this artist's image, zooms around its black-hole partner every 2.6 days.

Mistaken Identities?

But there's a catch. Black holes aren't the only things that can cause X-ray rings, multiple galaxy images, and whirling stars. When astronomers discover one of these clues, they have to be careful not to jump to conclusions.

And there's another challenge. Out in the universe, finding and interpreting X-ray signals, motion patterns, and other evidence can be tricky. Reality complicates the search. It's hard to get a detailed image, even with our best telescopes. Also, between a black hole and us is a lot of space, with galaxies, stardust, gases, and more. The clues are like footprints in a crowded forest—maybe you see them and can follow them, but maybe paw prints, branches, leaves, and shadows muddle the picture.

It takes a while for astronomers to sort through these complications. Once they spy a black-hole candidate, they get to work on the evidence. How does the candidate compare to what they expect from a black hole? Are there other ways to explain what they see? If the evidence lines up just so, astronomers move from being "pretty sure" to "almost positive" they've found a black hole.

That's how science can work. But sometimes, there are twists.

Quack!

You know the old scientific saying: If it looks like a duck, and quacks like a duck, then we can safely state it is likely to have its identity as a duck confirmed at some point in the future, pending additional evidence.

Supersized Surprises

A black hole is sometimes where you least expect it.

One unexpected twist came as a black-hole discovery that scientists never dreamed of. The story begins with a mystery from nearly a hundred years ago. For decades it seemed to have nothing to do with black holes. The story ends with a big—a really big!—surprise.

Radio Mysteries

In the 1930s a telephone-company engineer named Karl Jansky was trying to track down the cause of hissing static in phone lines when he discovered something strange. Radio energy from outer space was interfering with the phone signals. After learning about Janksy's discovery, a radio engineer named Grote Reber decided to investigate.

Star patterns light up the night and remind us of ancient myths. In the 1900s scientists discovered that some of these constellations held tantalizing clues to a bigger story. (Artist's representation)

What's the buzz?

Reber had just one little problem. To explore the radio energy, he needed a radio telescope—a telescope that could detect invisible radio energy—but there was no such thing at the time. So he invented one. He built it in his backyard in Wheaton, Illinois. Late into the night, Reber probed the sky with his new telescope, using it to locate the source of the mysterious radio energy.

Reber mapped these signals from the sky and shared his findings. Astronomers followed up with new investigations and soon began reporting more signals. Over time, with better radio telescopes, they found that some radio sources appeared as paired patches, one on either side of a tiny dot. They called these sources "radio galaxies." They also discovered other, more starlike sources—intense dots of radio energy without patches. How strange. What could these quasars (short for "quasi-stellar radio sources") be? Were they related to the radio galaxies?

In 1937 Grote Reber built this radio telescope from wood and sheet metal. His backyard wonder launched the study of invisible light energy from space.

Finally, in the early 1980s, improved images revealed a stunning new picture. The radio galaxies' patches were actually the ends of colossal streamers of energy, each one stretching hundreds of thousands of light years from the center. Something powerful had to be driving these gushing fountains of energy. And the quasars? They turned out to be far, far away, yet somehow creating radio impulses strong enough to reach Earth. No star could do this.

In fact, every quasar and radio galaxy dot turned out to be energy from the center of an entire galaxy. Astronomers found stars careening around these centers, zooming at previously unheard-of speeds in their orbits. The motion was like an accelerating ice skater pulled around her partner in a tight twirl—or like a fish caught in a superstrong whirlpool. Something extreme had to be in the middle of each of those galaxies.

In this false-color telescope image, lobes of radio energy shoot away from the center of the radio galaxy Cygnus A. Each enormous lobe is about 300,000 light years long.

As this artist's illustration shows, matter colliding near a supermassive black hole can kick up a ruckus of energy. Such energy "footprints" help scientists in their search for black holes.

You might be able to guess what this was, but for scientists, the best answer came as a shock. In 1994 telescopic evidence confirmed the amazing cause: a *supermassive* black hole, with the mass not of one imploded star, not of two, but of millions—maybe even billions.

Imagine the excitement! Scientists had discovered a new, entirely unexpected class of black holes when they weren't even looking for one. It was like playing hide-and-seek and tripping over a whole group of people you never knew were in the game.

As it turns out, supermassive black holes are probably at the heart of almost all galaxies, including our own.

Field Guide to Black Holes

Discoveries of black holes exploded in the late 1900s and early 2000s. What scientists found reads like a cast of characters for a mixed-up fairy tale. First they discovered the small ("Baby Bear") black holes, then the giant "Papas." But where were the medium "Mama Bear" black holes? It just didn't make sense that there would be smalls and larges but no mediums. Astronomers began the search, and found them. There's just one size that still hasn't been found, even though it has been predicted. The tiniest of all, the "Tom Thumbs" of the black-hole world, have yet to be discovered—if they even exist.

Who's been eating my porridge?

Size (in order of discovery)	What the pros call it	Has the same amount of mass as	Forms when
Small	Stellar-mass black hole	3–10 Suns	A large enough star ends, either in a supernova or by directly collapsing when it runs out of fuel.
Extra-extra-extra large	Supermassive black hole	Millions to billions of Suns	Stars, galaxies, and/or black holes collide? Huge gas clouds collapse? A smaller black hole grows as matter falls in over a long time? (Nobody's sure.)
Medium	Intermediate-mass black hole	100–10,000 Suns	Stars merge and then collapse? (People are mulling this over.)
Extra-extra-extra small—about the size of an atom, or smaller	Micro, mini, or primordial black hole	Mt. Everest	There's no evidence—yet—that these tiny black holes exist. If they do, they may have formed when the universe began, because of tiny imbalances of matter and energy.

Supermassive Start-Ups

We live in the Milky Way galaxy, far out on the edge of one of its spiral arms. Our part of the galaxy is relatively calm, but in the center is a supermassive black hole, a compaction of three million Suns' worth of matter.

This black hole is pretty mellow, as supermassive black holes go. Because its X-ray signal is relatively weak, astronomers didn't find it for a long time. They still don't know how it formed.

In fact, scientists are still puzzling over how any supermassive black hole gets started. Could a single supernova lead to one? Probably not. Even the biggest stars are much too puny to do the trick. To create a supermassive black hole, a star would have to start out millions of times the mass of the Sun. Astronomers think this is unlikely, so they have come up with other ideas. One idea has to do with crashing stars.

Near the center of a galaxy, stars are crammed relatively close together. As gravity swings them around each other, high-speed crashes are inevitable. Gravity can also cause entire galaxies to swerve together in intergalactic collisions.

When the huge amount of matter in colliding stars and galaxies compacts forcefully, it might form a mid-sized, or intermediate, black hole. With enough of this going on, several black holes might form and then pull

Our galaxy's central black hole is calm compared to others—but it still packs a wallop! Zooming in on the center of the Milky Way, we see a white hot spot that reveals the intensely energetic activity surrounding a supermassive black hole. (False-color telescope image)

You are here

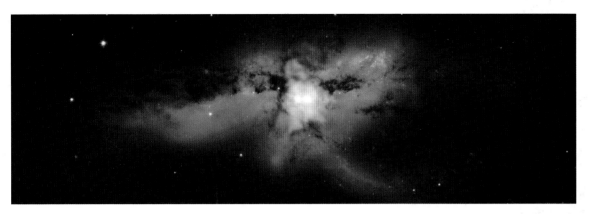

Deep in the center of the galaxy NGC 6240, two unseen supermassive black holes are merging in a slow-motion collision. The "crash" began thirty million years ago and may continue for another hundred million years or more. The collision creates a bright splash of X-ray energy, captured here in false color.

together, morphing into one. Nearby stars might also spiral into these growing black holes, adding to the total mass. Over time, all this piling up might lead to a supermassive black hole.

Radio galaxies, quasars, supermassive black holes—in less than one hundred years, we've made many discoveries about black holes. The theory works and the evidence is good. The conclusions seem sound.

But still . . . all of this evidence is like guessing what's inside a gift box but not being able to open it. If you could, wouldn't you want to peek inside the package and see for yourself? Wouldn't you want to visit a black hole?

Tomorrow's News

It seems that every time you turn around, astronomers are discovering something new about space. But this wasn't always the case, especially with black holes. It took several decades to go from thinking black holes could be possible to actually tracking one down.

Compare that to what's been happening more recently. Within the past decade or so, scientists confirmed that supermassive black holes exist and figured out they must be at the center of most galaxies. Astronomers found intermediate black holes, and discovered the first solo stellar-mass black holes—ones without visible partner stars. And they have tracked matter falling into a distant black hole and determined just how a black hole propels its super-energetic jets.

The fact is, you've been alive during some of the most exciting times in black-hole astronomy. Just imagine what scientists may discover by the time you're twenty!

Stay tuned . . .

Meet the Neighbors (and Then Some): Getting to Know a Few Black Holes

Thousands of objects either seem likely to be black holes or have reached "almost positive" confirmation as black holes. Which ones are closest? Smallest? Biggest? Here are some black-hole highlights.

Sagittarius A*

(Read this as "Sagittarius A star.")

Type: Supermassive

Importance: The black hole at the center of our galaxy

Location: The center of the Milky Way galaxy, which is 27 thousand light years away, in the constellation Sagittarius

Cool fact: Today we know that Sagittarius A* is one of the mysterious radio sources that Grote Reber discovered with his homemade telescope. It is 4 million times the mass of the Sun.

NGC 5128

(Also known as Centaurus A)

Type: Supermassive

Importance: The black hole in the center of our nearest active galaxy

Location: About 14 million light years away, in the constellation Centaurus

Cool fact: At 200 million times the mass of the Sun, this black hole is far more massive than Sagittarius A*.

V4641 Sagittarii

(Also known as V4641 Sgr)

Type: Stellar mass

Importance: One of the closest known black holes to Earth

Location: 1,600 light years away, in the constellation Sagittarius

Cool fact: V4641 Sagittarii is actually a binary system with one visible star and one black hole circling each other.

(Artist's representation)

NGC 4486

(Also known as Virgo A)

Type: Supermassive

Importance: One of the biggest of the biggest!

Location: 50 million light years away, in the constellation Virgo

Cool fact: This black hole is really huge! The distance from one side of its event horizon to the other is about the same distance across as Pluto's orbit. It has an estimated mass of 3 billion times that of the Sun.

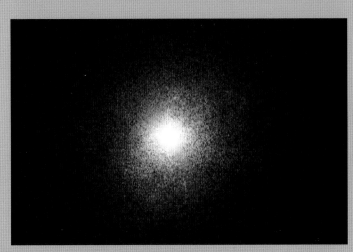

Cygnus X-1

Type: Stellar mass

Importance: One of the smallest known black holes. Also, one of the first-ever black-hole candidates.

Location: About 6,000–8,000 light years away, in the "heart" of the constellation Cygnus

Cool fact: This black hole is so small that it would take less than an hour to drive the distance across it.

Close Encounters of the Imaginary Kind

A black hole is a destination—

for your imagination.

Unfortunately for the curious traveler, actually visiting a black hole in the near future is downright impossible. Even the nearest black holes are too far away.

For example, one of Earth's closest black-hole "neighbors" is about 1,600 light years away. (That's about 9 quadrillion miles, or 14 quadrillion kilometers.) No spacecraft is going to get you to a black hole and back by dinnertime—even if you live to be one hundred and only want dinner on your last day.

Luckily, you can visit a black hole with your imagination. Fueled by facts, you can blast off to a black hole or two and find out what might happen once you arrive.

The Closest‡ Black Hole to Earth?

If you were to aim a powerful-enough flashlight at the Moon right now, the light would reach it in a little more than a second—maybe before you got to the end of this sentence. And how long would it take for light to reach our nearest known black-hole neighbor, called V4641 Sagittarii? Fifty *billion* seconds. If you aimed your flashlight in its direction, toward the constellation Sagittarius, the light would arrive there sometime around the year 3600.

‡Because black-hole science is booming, by the time you read this there may be a newly discovered black hole that's even closer to Earth than V4641 Sagittarii.

What might happen to a spaceship approaching a black hole? (Artist's representation)

Are we there yet?

49

A Hole Variety of Places to Visit

As you take off, remember: predicting the exact details of your journey is tricky. After all, no one has ever visited a black hole, and we can't send a probe in to take a peek and send the information back to us. Not even sneak previews can escape from a black hole.

However, scientists have some best guesses about what could happen, based on what they know about gravity and black holes. A helpful rule of thumb is that close to the center of any black hole, every inch matters. Just a short distance can make an enormous difference in the strength of the black hole's gravitational effects.

The particulars of your adventure also depend on the type of black hole you visit. What size is it? Is it lumpy or smooth? Maybe it's a spinner?

Wish you were here!

Greetings From Cygnus X-1!

A spectacular view . . .

. . . of NGC 4486

Spinners, Lumpies, and Smoothies

When it comes to black holes, matter really matters. After all, if it weren't for all the matter crunched into a tiny space, an extreme gravity zone could never form. But it's not just *how much* matter in how small a space that makes a difference. *How* a star's matter collapses also affects the black hole that forms.

If the star was spinning before the collapse, then the black hole will spin, too. If the collapse is perfectly symmetric, a smooth black hole forms. On the other hand, even a slightly lopsided collapse leads to a lumpy black hole, with erratic gravitational effects. The gravity might be strong in some places and weak in others, and pull in different directions. However, a lumpy hole won't stay lumpy for long, because its own gravity will work to smooth it out.

Beyond Your Brainy Blast-Off:
Journey to a Black Hole

Suppose you were to visit a perfectly symmetric, smallish, non-spinning black hole. What would happen? Right away, you would need a new nickname—something like Stretch or the Spaghetti Kid. The pull from the black hole would force your body into a long, skinny, stringy shape. If you were going in feet first, your feet would stretch out the most. For a moment, they might look like droopy wet socks.

Not that you would notice any of this. By the time your toes could register "ouch" in your brain, your brain would not be working. This is the one time when stretching your mind might be a bad idea.

What if the black hole were lumpy? Instead of getting a nice, smooth stretch, you'd be pushed and pulled in changing directions, like human dough in a wrestling match with a pretzel maker. (The pretzel maker wins.)

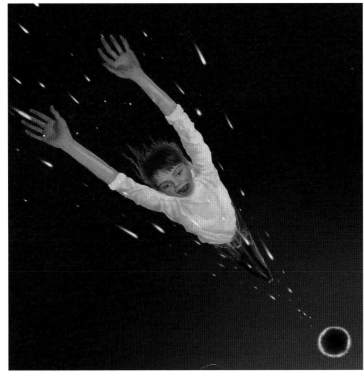

A kid visiting a black hole might be stretched out like spaghetti. Scientists call this phenomenon spaghettification, or the noodle effect. (Artist's representation)

Approaching the event horizon

After crossing the event horizon

(Artist's representations)

So much for experiencing a smallish black hole; you'd have no time for sightseeing. A visit to a bigger black hole could be more interesting. It might take a while for the major effects to kick in. As you drifted in from the event horizon toward the singularity at the center, you might get a chance to look around.

What might you see? Even before you crossed the event horizon, things would start to look strange. The black hole would bend the light from all around and focus it in a miniature picture. Instead of seeing a sky full of stars, you'd see a tiny image of the black hole's surroundings, focused smack dab in the middle of the blackness overhead. Even stars on the opposite side of the black hole would be visible above you.

After you crossed the event horizon, the warped-sky image would distort even more. Now the light from everything outside the black hole would form a ring above you, like a halo overhead. Your sky would appear dark except for that bright circle—a ribbon of light that would get skinnier and skinnier as you continued to zoom inward.

You might want to tell the folks back home about this. Ah, well, too bad. Once across the event horizon, you wouldn't be able to get out any blogs or vlogs, email or phone calls, snail mail, smoke signals, messages in bottles, or signal flares to spread the news.

It would be as if you were stuck in a one-way, sight-proof, soundproof bubble, sealed away from the rest of the universe. But there's no sense letting this tear you up. In a few hours, gravity will do the job instead.

Hmmm. Maybe you'd better turn that imagination of yours around and head back to Earth. That's the thing about thought experiments: they let you experience the impossible—and still get home in time for dinner.

Can you hear me now?

Well, usually. One of the best-ever thought experimenters missed more than a meal or two while on his mental adventures. "I am often so engrossed in my work that I forget to eat lunch," he wrote in a letter to his eleven-year-old son, just days before he unveiled one of his biggest ideas to a group of scientists. And what an engrossing, even bizarre idea it was! It took scientists on an incredible journey—a fantastic voyage through space and time that eventually led to black holes.

Ultimate FX?‡

Careening toward a singularity, you might have a colorful experience, if only for a blink of an eye. Picture the colors in a rainbow. Add the invisible light on either side—such as low-level infrared energy beyond red and high-energy X-rays beyond blue. Got it?

Now forget it. Viewed from in and near a black hole, colors can undergo some shifty effects, sliding from the red side of the rainbow toward the blue.

Yellow, green, and blue stars disappear—until you spot them with your X-ray detector. Meanwhile, new "stars" wink into view—balls of gas that glow in shifted infrared. Why? Light is distorted as it passes between places with different gravitation. The greater the difference, the greater the distortion. A black hole's extreme gravity intensifies this effect to the max.

Invisible radio, microwave, and infrared		Invisible ultraviolet, X-ray, and gamma

What you normally see: yellow → What you see from a black hole: nothing

The color of the star shifts as you approach the extreme gravity zone of the black hole. (Diagram not to scale)

Now try this tasty thought experiment. Say some friends far outside the black hole decide to send you a snack. If they launch a red apple your way, it's invisible to you at first. But keep your eyes peeled! Eventually, the apple shifts from invisible to blue, then to green, yellow, orange, and finally red, as it passes through gravitational zones that are closer and closer to the same strength as yours. Quick! Grab that apple before it disappears! Remember, once it whizzes past you, all its light continues in one direction, toward the center of the black hole, and you won't see it anymore.

‡ Predictions like these are iffy. They are based on what scientists know about light and gravity. And they might be right—if the known laws of physics don't break down past the event horizon.

Turning the Universe Upside-Down

A black hole is part of a strange new universe.

The scientist who forgot to eat his lunch was busy cooking up a whole new way of thinking about gravity. He was a radical smarty-pants—somebody with a wild imagination. Someone whose brain could surprise even himself.

Albert Einstein didn't *mean* to turn the universe upside-down on everyone. He didn't *plan* on leading others to discover black holes. At first, all he set out to do was think about motion, along with a few other related ideas. But almost before he knew it, he had suddenly made our dependable old universe seem strange and new.

Just imagine being on an alien world and catching this view of a black hole in the night sky! Imagination has always helped open the door to new ideas in science. In fact, imagination led scientists to the idea of black holes. (Artist's representation)

Einstein's Spacey Ideas

Before Einstein, everyone pretty much thought of space as a sort of blank nothingness that separated objects like planets, solar systems, stars, and galaxies. This nothingness of space was a humongous, rigid background, with all of the matter in the universe arranged on it like pieces on a game board. Newton's force of gravity ruled this game, pulling things closer together and making them move against the spacey backdrop of nothingness.

But Einstein had his own ideas.

What if this background wasn't rigid? What if it wasn't nothingness?

What if it didn't stay the same all the time? What if, instead, space itself was something that changes—and even reacts to masses and matter?

Thanks to Einstein, we can imagine space as a blanket that stretches in response to every object's mass. A more massive object, such as the Earth, makes a deeper depression than a less massive object, such as the Moon. (Diagram not to scale)

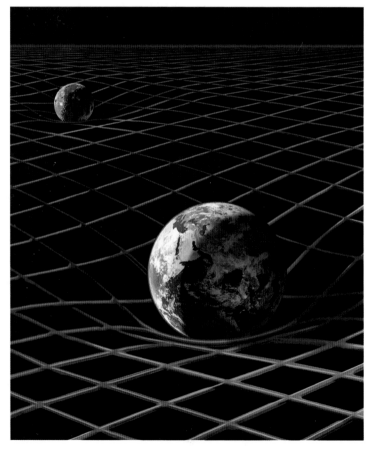

In this way of thinking, the "background" acted more like a flexible mat, or a stretchy knit blanket. This new, blanket-like idea of space meant space could stretch, crunch up, bend, and warp. Moving objects would follow the curves of the blanket, moving along the surface through flat sections as well as distorted ones. This new idea about space changed the way scientists think about gravity.

Speaking of Gravity: Newtonese and Einsteinese

Most of the time gravity *seems* to work the way Newton described it. Newton's rules explain a lot, from falling apples to most planets' orbits. But his laws don't work perfectly. In high-gravity zones, Newton's ideas don't jibe with what scientists observe. For example, Mercury's orbit—up close to the Sun—has a blip in it that Newton's laws can't explain.

Glitches like this one were the reason Einstein worked so hard at coming up with a new explanation. He wanted to account for everything. His ideas about curving space may sound bizarre, but they work! They took care of the gaps in Newton's theory and explained Mercury's orbit. They led scientists to predict shifting starlight and black holes. All of this is powerful evidence that Einstein was on to something.

However, in day-to-day experience, the strangeness of Einstein's ideas doesn't help us, and Newton's notions do just fine. In everyday life, when gravity isn't especially intense, Newton's and Einstein's ways of thinking lead to similar results. The two explanations work like different languages that express the same thing. Is an apple red (English) or *rojo* (Spanish)? It's okay to use either description.

So we still use Newton's laws—even scientists do, much of the time. Sure, it's more exact to be Einsteinian and think of gravity as matter's effect on space. But it's all right to take a Newtonian shortcut and imagine gravity as a pull.

57

Gravity:
A Real Mind—and Space—Bender

In Einstein's way of thinking, what we see as gravitational "attraction" between two objects isn't really the effect of those objects pulling on each other. Instead, gravity is the effect that matter has on space itself.

Any material in space causes a distortion of some sort. A small concentration of matter results in a tiny dimple. A higher concentration makes a deeper dent. Each indentation is the gravity zone around the object.

Near the object, the distortion is greatest. The stretchy threads of the space fabric are bent by the effect of the mass on space. Farther and farther away, this effect is smaller and smaller, and so the threads are straighter and straighter.

A peanut would form a shallow dimple. If you could squash two peanuts together so they took up the same space as one, the dent would be slightly deeper. The deeper the dent, the steeper the gravity zone. It would take more energy for things to get out of the deeper dent.

From Einstein's Gravity to Black Holes

Einstein's idea of gravity had big consequences. It helped explain some observations that Newton's idea didn't account for. It also opened our minds to amazing new possibilities. For example, taking his cue from Einstein's idea that space bends, scientist Karl Schwarzschild began to think about what would happen if a place in space were extremely distorted. His answer: light would follow the hyper-bent space, never to turn away from it. This was the first prediction of a black hole. At first, some scientists (including Einstein!) rejected Schwarzschild's ideas. Others were intrigued and began searching the skies for real black holes. Just decades later, they found the first of them. It just goes to show: sometimes, as Einstein himself once said, "Imagination is more important than knowledge."

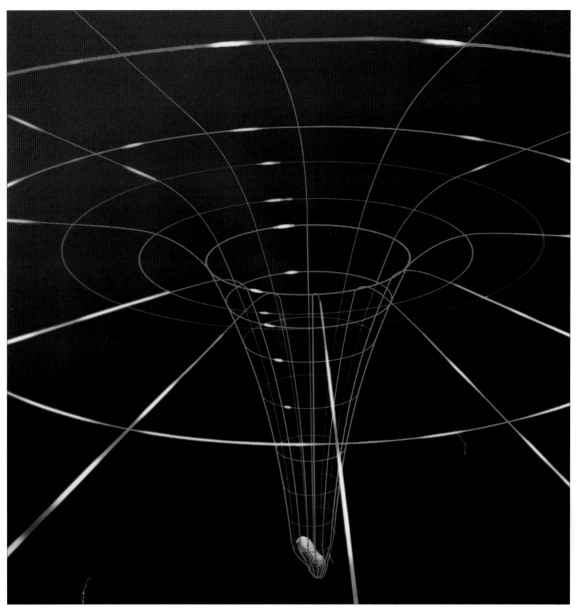

An elephant-packed peanut would be small and magnificently massive. It would cause a deep dent in the fabric of space. (Diagram not to scale)

The dense singularity at a black hole's center would be an extremely tiny but extremely heavy object placed on the blanket. Picture the supernova leftovers—the material that originally forms a black hole—as a peanut with all of the elephants in the world stuffed into it. Imagine placing that tremendously dense, elephant-stuffed peanut on a huge blanket. The blanket stretches and stretches, pulling out of shape. It forms not a shallow dimple in the blanket, but a steep well. A steep well that's really a lot like . . .

. . . a hole!

Glowing gas and dust whirl around a black hole. As they follow the dramatic curve in the fabric of space, they spiral along the steep gravity well that leads to the dense singularity at the center of the black hole. (Artist's representation)

So . . .
Even though a black hole is
NOT a hole—
at least not the kind you
can poke your finger through
or dig in the ground—
a black hole is NOT
exactly NOT a hole, either.

Is it?

Time Line

Discovering Black Holes

It took a lot to discover black holes—lots of brain power, time, and technology. Here are just a few of the major milestones. You may notice something about this history. In the early days, most of the folks leading the way were men from Europe or the United States. Now that's changing, as men and women from around the world continue to share in the excitement of discovery.

Sometime in the distant past

For the very first time, somebody doesn't just *notice* falling, but wonders about it. People from different cultures try to explain it—and keep trying until . . .

1687

English scientist and mathematician Isaac Newton writes about his ideas on gravity. He says it's a force that pulls objects together. (See pages 13–15.)

1783

1798

Separately, British scientist John Michell (in 1783) and French scientist Pierre-Simon Laplace (in 1798) speculate about Newton's idea of gravity and come up with an idea that people will later call "dark stars"—stars so massive that their light cannot shine out. (This notion is close to the idea of a black hole, but different.)

Late 1800s

By now scientists realize that Newton's rules for gravity don't explain everything. (For example, the planet Mercury doesn't move the way Newton's theory predicts.)

1905

German-born Swiss (and later American) scientist Albert Einstein publishes his ideas on time, space, and motion, which will lead to thinking about gravity in new ways.

1915

Albert Einstein skips meals while putting the finishing touches on his full theory of gravity and motion, called the theory of general relativity. It includes a big idea: gravity is not a force! It just looks that way, because matter bends space. (See pages 56–59.)

1916

Karl Schwarzschild, a German scientist, is the first to see that if Einstein is right, black holes may exist—but he doesn't call them black holes. (See page 58.)

1919

Arthur Eddington from England and his international team of scientists observe that gravity can change the path of light, as predicted by Einstein's theory of general relativity. This is strong evidence that Einstein is on to something. (So Schwarzschild might be, too.) (See page 30.)

1933

American engineer Karl Jansky announces that radio waves are coming from outer space— and messing up phone lines, making them hiss. (See page 39.)

1939

Einstein writes about why he thinks Schwarzschild's proposed objects "do not exist." He rejects the idea of black holes!

Meanwhile, American scientists J. Robert Oppenheimer and Hartland Snyder figure out that some collapsing stars could lead to what we now call black holes.

1944

After years of studying the skies with his homemade radio telescope, American engineer Grote Reber begins publishing maps of the mysterious radio energy from outer space. The energy sources will later be known as radio galaxies. (See pages 39–40.)

1953

Using more powerful telescopes, Roger Jennison from the UK and Mrinal Das Gupta from India observe that Reber's energy sources are paired patches of radio energy around radio centers. (See page 40.)

1960

American scientists Allan Sandage and Thomas A. Matthews discover and photograph the first of a new type of strange radio object—later named a quasar. (See page 40.)

1963

Dutch-born Maarten Schmidt and American Jesse Greenstein realize that radio galaxies and quasars are very far away and must be emitting tremendous amounts of energy. (See page 41.)

1964

Somebody—nobody can remember who—uses the term "black holes" at a scientific meeting. It doesn't catch on.

For the first time, scientists propose how to search for clues that would lead to a black hole (though they still don't call it that). The scientists are Yakov Zel'dovich and Oktay Guseinov (both from the Soviet Union) and Edwin Salpeter (an Austrian-Australian-American).

Zel'dovich and Salpeter suggest that something with a tremendous amount of mass may be powering the energy from quasars and radio galaxies. (See page 41.)

1967

American scientist John A. Wheeler starts using the snappy phrase "black holes" to mean "gravitationally completely collapsed stars"—and this time the name catches on.

1969

British scientist Donald Lynden-Bell proposes that supermassive black holes may be the power source behind quasars and radio galaxies.

1971

The first possible black holes are identified with the help of X-ray telescope Uhuru. Observations of radio and visible light provide supporting evidence. One of the candidates is Cygnus X-1, orbiting a visible star. (See page 47.)

British scientist Stephen Hawking proposes that tiny black holes may exist. (These are later called micro, mini, or primordial black holes.) (See page 43.)

1994

Measurements confirm the possibility of supermassive black holes. The "proof"? Using the Hubble Space Telescope, scientists led by Americans Richard Harms and Holland Ford find a disk of gas whipping around the center of galaxy M87. The gas is moving so fast that only a supermassive black hole—or some other, unknown object—can be at the center. (See page 42.)

1999

After lots of study, astronomers begin to agree: evidence suggests that most galaxies have a supermassive black hole at their center.

2001

American scientist Joseph F. Dolan announces the first observations of matter spiraling into a black hole, discovered by comparing two years of Hubble Space Telescope data from Cygnus X-1.

2002–2003

Finally! Thanks to new evidence collected and reported by several teams— including those led by Andrea Ghez and by German scientists Reinhard Genzel, Thomas Ott, and Rainer Schödel— scientists are generally convinced that a supermassive black hole is at the heart of the Milky Way. (See page 44.)

The present

You shine a flashlight out toward the nearest known black hole— V4641 Sagittarii in the direction of the constellation Sagittarius. (See page 49.)

3600
(Give or take a few years)

If the flashlight beam is strong enough and nothing interrupts its path, the light from the present arrives at V4641 Sagittarii and crosses the event horizon.

2000

For the first time, observations reveal a "lone" stellar-mass black hole—like what Schwarzschild predicted in 1916. Before this, stellar-mass black holes had been found only as part of binary star systems.

2000

X-ray evidence reveals the first intermediate-mass black hole. (It's in the galaxy called M82.)

2000

Meanwhile, a team led by American scientist Andrea Ghez announces an extraordinary finding: some amazing force is whipping stars faster and faster around the center of the Milky Way. Each year the stars' speeds increase by about 250,000 miles (more than 400,000 kilometers) per hour! The team concludes that a supermassive black hole can explain this—but not everyone else agrees.

65

Glossary

Atom: The smallest amount you can have of a basic material, such as the smallest possible amount of copper in a penny. Every atom has a central part, called the nucleus, and one or more outer particles, called electrons.

Binary star: Two stars that orbit around each other. From far away, without a telescope, the two stars can look like one.

Black hole: A place in space with an extremely strong gravity zone that surrounds very dense matter in the center. The gravitational effect is so strong that once in this zone, nothing can exit—not even light.

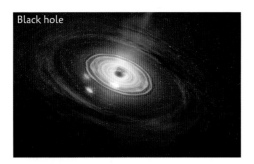
Black hole

Constellation: A pattern of stars in the night sky that people have noticed and named. Although a constellation may look like a dot-to-dot drawing on a flat sheet of paper, its stars may be at very different distances from Earth. When we say that something is "in a constellation," that means it shows up in the same part of the sky as that star pattern.

Electron: One of the types of particles that make up an atom. Electrons are found outside the atom's nucleus.

Energy: The capacity to make things happen. For example, it takes energy to shake things up, heat them, and make them move. Energy comes in different forms, like sound, motion, visible light, X-rays, radio waves, and heat.

Event horizon: The boundary around a black hole that acts like a point of no return. Outside the boundary, it is possible for things to move away from the black hole. From inside the boundary, nothing can get back out.

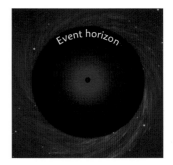
Event horizon

Fallback: One of the ways in which a black hole can form. Fallback happens after a supernova, when leftover star material falls back on itself in a sudden collapse, crunching together into a tight singularity.

False-color image: In astronomy, a color-coded map, often produced by a telescope. In telescope images, the colors represent light signals that are normally invisible to the human eye, such as radio waves and X-rays.

False-color image

Force: Any push or pull.

Friction: The motion of objects against each other, which results in their heating up. It can also mean a force that resists the motion of objects against each other.

Fusion: Melding, or blending two or more things to make one thing. Nuclear fusion happens when two atoms' centers (nuclei) are forced together and become one new nucleus. Fusing atoms can release a tremendous amount of energy. This energy is what keeps a star burning.

Galaxy: A group of billions and billions of stars, clustered together because of their gravitational effect on each other.

Galaxy

Gravitas: The Latin name Isaac Newton used for gravity.

Gravitational lensing: A distorting effect that intense gravity can have on light. Gravitational lensing can make an image appear to be split, stretched, or multiplied.

Gravity: 1. According to Newton's theory, a naturally occurring pulling force between any two objects. 2. According to Einstein's theory, the bending effect that any matter has on the space around it, causing other matter to move toward it.

Intermediate black hole: A black hole with a mass that is more than ten times but less than millions of times the mass of the Sun.

Light: A form of energy. Light can be visible to human eyes, as in sunlight, or invisible, as in infrared light, radio waves, and X-rays.

Light year: The distance light can travel in one year, which is about 6 trillion miles (more than 9.5 trillion kilometers).

Mass: 1. The amount of material, matter, or substance that something contains. 2. Another word for matter.

Matter: Stuff, substance, or material.

Micro black hole, mini black hole, or primordial black hole: A microscopic black hole. Scientists think microscopic black holes may exist but have not found any (yet).

Neutron: One of the types of particles in the nucleus of an atom. Neutrons are also found in neutron stars.

Neutron star: An extremely dense star made of neutrons. A neutron star forms after the supernova phase of a very heavy star that is not quite massive enough to form a black hole. (The only thing known to be denser than a neutron star is a black hole.)

Neutron star

Nuclear reaction: A high-energy interaction that takes place in or between atomic nuclei. One type of nuclear reaction, fusion, is what causes a star to shine.

Nuclei: The plural form of the word *nucleus*. Pronounced *NOO-klee-eye.*

Nucleus (of an atom): The tiny center part of an atom, containing small particles called protons and neutrons. A nucleus usually repels other nuclei.

Plasma: A very energetic form (or state) of matter. (Solid, liquid, and gas are other states of matter.) Plasma is found in stars, among other places. Like a liquid or gas, plasma has no definite shape and can move and flow freely. Plasma forms when a lot of energy is added to a gas, causing the electrons in its atoms to separate from their nuclei.

Quasar: A type of space object discovered in the 1960s with radio telescopes. The name "quasar" comes from the term "quasi-stellar radio source," meaning a radio source that seems *almost* like a star—but not quite. Scientists now think that each quasar is the energy streaming away from a supermassive black hole at the center of a galaxy. See *radio galaxy.*

Radio: A type of invisible light energy.

Radio galaxy

Radio galaxy: A type of space object first mapped in the 1940s with radio signals. Radio galaxies are now known to be galaxies, each with a supermassive black hole at its center and energy streaming off in opposite directions. Today radio galaxies' streamers of energy are thought to be the same thing as quasars, just seen from a different angle. (When we observe a radio galaxy, we are likely seeing a side-view of the streamers. A quasar is thought to be the head-on view.) See *quasar.*

Radio telescope: A telescope that works by detecting invisible radio waves instead of visible light. Based on the radio signals, radio telescopes create visible images, allowing people to see otherwise invisible information.

Sagittarius A*: The name given to the radio source at the center of the Milky Way galaxy, now known to be a black hole. Pronounced *saj-ih-TAIR-ee-us ay star.*

Sagittarius A*

Singularity: The single point at the center of a black hole where all of its tremendously dense matter is concentrated. The rest of the black hole is the powerful gravity zone that surrounds this tiny spot.

Spaghettification: The stretching of any object into a long, skinny, spaghetti-like shape as it approaches a black hole. Sometimes called the noodle effect.

Star: A large, extremely hot ball of glowing gas and plasma.

Stellar: Having to do with stars.

Stellar-mass black hole: A black hole that forms when a massive star runs out of fuel. The original star is as massive as twenty-five to one hundred Suns, and the black hole it forms has three to ten times the mass of the Sun.

Supermassive black hole: A giant black hole—millions or billions of times the mass of the Sun—thought possibly to form from collisions of stars, galaxies, or smaller black holes, or a combination of these.

Supernova: 1. The end phase of some stars, which takes place after nuclear fusion stops. A supernova involves an inward collapse of star material, followed by a giant rebound, which makes the star seem extra bright and large from a distance. When conditions are right, a supernova becomes a black hole. 2. The event that takes place when a star becomes a supernova. You can talk about a star "going supernova" or say that a supernova is happening.

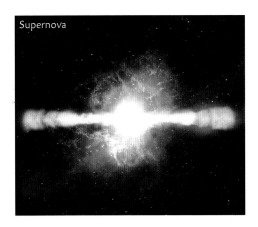
Supernova

Thought experiment: A sort of mind game scientists play in order to think through their ideas about how the universe works. Thought experiments can be especially useful when it would be difficult or impossible to run a real-life experiment. The scientist imagines a set of circumstances and then tries to figure out what would happen next. For example, a scientist might ask, "What would happen if a person could visit a black hole and survive? What would that person see?"

V4641 Sagittarii (or V4641 Sgr): The name of the closest known black hole to Earth, about 1,600 light years away in the direction of the constellation Sagittarius. "Sagittarii" is pronounced *saj-ih-TAIR-ee-eye.*

V4641 Sagittarii

White dwarf: The cooling end phase of stars that do not become supernovas. They are called white dwarfs because they appear to be dim, whitish objects. Close up, white dwarfs are intensely bright. However, because they are small, they don't seem bright from far away.

X-ray: A highly energetic form of light that is invisible to human eyes.

X-ray telescope: A telescope that works by detecting invisible X-rays instead of visible light. Based on the X-ray signals, X-ray telescopes create visible images, allowing people to see otherwise invisible information.

Chandra X-ray telescope

Author's Note

How Do You Know I Know?

Whenever you read nonfiction, it's a good idea to check and see what the author has to say about how he or she found out about the topic. It helps you figure out how reliable the information is. (However, even reliable work gets outdated—especially in science, where new information and discoveries can take surprising turns.)

So, where did I find my facts and figures? In lots of different places. Tracking down information about black holes was a little like tracking black holes themselves. It took research, questions, and lots of cross-checking to piece together something that made sense. Then again, it was a lot easier for me to track down information than it is for astronomers to locate black holes—thanks to high-quality Internet resources and helpful librarians, such as Jeffrey Mehigan and Debbie Batson. Luckily I was able to find what I wanted without special X-ray detectors.

You know you've used a book a lot when you find cookie crumbs in the binding. Right now, my most-crumb-filled book is *Black Holes & Time Warps: Einstein's Outrageous Legacy* by the scientist and science writer Kip Thorne.

I found lots of great information in science magazines, such as *Scientific American, Astronomy,* and *Sky and Telescope.* These led me to other useful resources. When it was time to get to the details, I looked at scientists' reports, along with summaries of the reports, in scientific journals.

It's terrific fun to read what the original thinkers had to say for themselves. I read parts of *Relativity: The Special and General Theory* by Albert Einstein, and found the letter about Einstein forgetting to eat lunch in *Einstein: His Life and Universe* by Walter Isaacson.

I also reviewed parts of Isaac Newton's *Principia: The Mathematical Principles of Natural Philosophy* (translated by Andrew Motte), to see what Newton himself had to say.

I try to be careful about how I use websites. As you probably already know, not all of them have reliable information. But to point me in good directions or answer specific questions, I checked out numerous articles at SpaceRef:

www.spaceref.com

I loved every page of the Chandra X-ray Observatory's site on black holes:

http://chandra.harvard.edu/xray_sources/blackholes.html

NASA's fact sheets on solar-system objects were helpful, too:

http://nssdc.gsfc.nasa.gov/planetary/

It's also important for me to talk to people who understand science. For this book, that included my husband, friends, and Dr. Wendy Hagen Bauer, professor of astronomy at Wellesley College. Dr. Bauer graciously agreed to serve as my expert reader. Her dedication and attention to detail were impressive. I am grateful to her and to the other scientists she talked with as she helped me.

Of course, even with all these resources and helpful people, I may have made errors. If they exist, I hope they are few and far between, but if you find any, they are mine, all mine!

Resources

Books

Asimov, Isaac. *How Did We Find Out About Black Holes?* New York: Walker and Company, 1978.
This oldy is still a goody. Isaac Asimov writes in clear detail about key discoveries related to black holes.

Burnham, Robert. *The Reader's Digest Children's Atlas of the Universe.* New York: Reader's Digest Children's Books, 2000.
Who wouldn't want to explore a book chock-full of information and images about the universe?

Hollihan, Kerrie Logan. *Isaac Newton and Physics for Kids: His Life and Ideas with 21 Activities.* Chicago: Chicago Review Press, 2009.
This book will take you beyond gravity into Newton's other groundbreaking ideas, proving he truly was a wise guy.

Jackson, Ellen. *The Mysterious Universe: Supernovae, Dark Energy, and Black Holes.* Boston: Houghton Mifflin, 2008.
The universe has room for lots of cool phenomena.

MacLeod, Elizabeth. *Albert Einstein: A Life of Genius.* Toronto: Kids Can Press, 2003.
Find out about Einstein and his ideas in this biography.

Websites

The websites listed below were current at the time of publication. To find out more about black holes, try searching for "black hole" using your favorite search engine.

Chandra X-ray Observatory
http://chandra.harvard.edu
Marvel at images of supernovae and other intergalactic wonders exposed by the X-ray vision of the Chandra telescope.

HubbleSite: Black Holes
http://hubblesite.org/explore_astronomy/black_holes/
Explore the Black Hole Encyclopedia, take an animated trip to a black hole, and use special tools to scope out X-ray and radio "sights" in the night sky.

NASA's Imagine the Universe!
http://imagine.gsfc.nasa.gov/docs/science/science.html
Dig deeper into the physics and astronomy of black holes (and more).

StarDate's Black Hole Encyclopedia
http://blackholes.stardate.org/
Keep up with tomorrow's news with this online encyclopedia of black holes, published by the McDonald Observatory at the University of Texas at Austin.

Starship Asterisk*
http://asterisk.apod.com/viewtopic.php?f=8&t=23207&start=25
Watch an animation of stars orbiting the black hole at the center of our galaxy.

Image Credits

Index

Poodlena

To my dog, Max and my sister, Victoria

BLOOMSBURY
CHILDREN'S
BOOKS

Type set in Mona Lisa
The art was done in gouache

Published by Bloomsbury, New York and London
Distributed to the trade by Holtzbrinck Publishers
Library of Congress Cataloging-in-Publication Data
McHenry, E. B.
Poodlena / by E. B. McHenry
p. cm.
Summary: Poodlena Pompadour, a perfectly-groomed pink poodle,
discovers the joys of playing in a muddy dog park.
ISBN 1-58234-824-3 (alk. paper)
[1. Poodles—Fiction. 2. Dogs—Fiction. 3. Grooming—Fiction.
4. Behavior—Fiction. 5. Stories in rhyme.] I. Title.
PZ8.M1597 Po 2003
[E]—dc21
2002028347

First U.S. Edition

1 3 5 7 9 10 8 6 4 2

Bloomsbury USA Children's Books
175 Fifth Avenue
New York, New York 10010

Printed in Hong Kong/China

Poodlena

by E. B. McHenry

BLOOMSBURY
CHILDREN'S
BOOKS

In a big-city high-rise
On the very top floor
Lived a pink, fluffy poodle—
Poodlena Pompadour.

She wore on her head
A pink mountain of hair,
As light as a feather,
And mostly pink air.

Days were spent teasing her fabulous fluff—
Shaving legs, painting toenails, and other such stuff.

It took lots of work, and a good bit of spray,
To look pretty and perfect in just the right way.

She'd fuss and she'd tweeze,

She'd paint and she'd fluff,

She'd powder, perfume,

And pink herself up.

When finally finished,
Leashed, late in the day,
She'd leave for the park
For the dog time to play.

Down, down she'd go
At three quarters past four,
To the elegant lobby
From the very top floor.

From the elegant lobby, out revolving glass doors,
Through rush-hour traffic, past big-city stores.

At five she'd arrive
To a wild dog park scene

Where dogs whizzed around
Fetching balls on the green.

But she kept far away
From their ball-fetching jaws,
Away from wet noses,
And mud-padded paws.

Safe on the sidewalk,
All fluffed, pink, and clean,
Never running or sniffing,
Wanting just to be seen.

One night storm clouds blew in,
Heavy rains filled the sky.
No dog park for days—
She stayed in, clean and dry.

She fussed and she tweezed,

She painted and fluffed,

She powdered, perfumed,

And pinked herself up.

When the rain finally stopped
She returned to the scene
And arrived extra pink,
Extra fluffed up, and clean.

But disaster had struck—
The park was afloat.
Mud covered the sidewalk—
It looked like a moat.

The mud was a river, an ocean, a sea.
She felt kind of itchy, did she feel a flea?

She did feel a flea, in fact she felt three—
Stopping to scratch, she was hit!

Suddenly...

She flew up in the air,
Spinning round and around,
Getting covered in mud
As she slid to the ground.

Her mountain of hair
Hung soggy and small,
Her pink, perfect look
Somehow lost in the fall.

Woozy but wagging,
Shaken up but not down,
She was chased by a chow—
So she chased him around!

She raced after balls—
Fetching more than a few,
Staying late, playing games
Till all vanished from view.

With so many balls
To be fetched in a day,
Now she fluffs a bit less
And makes more time to play.

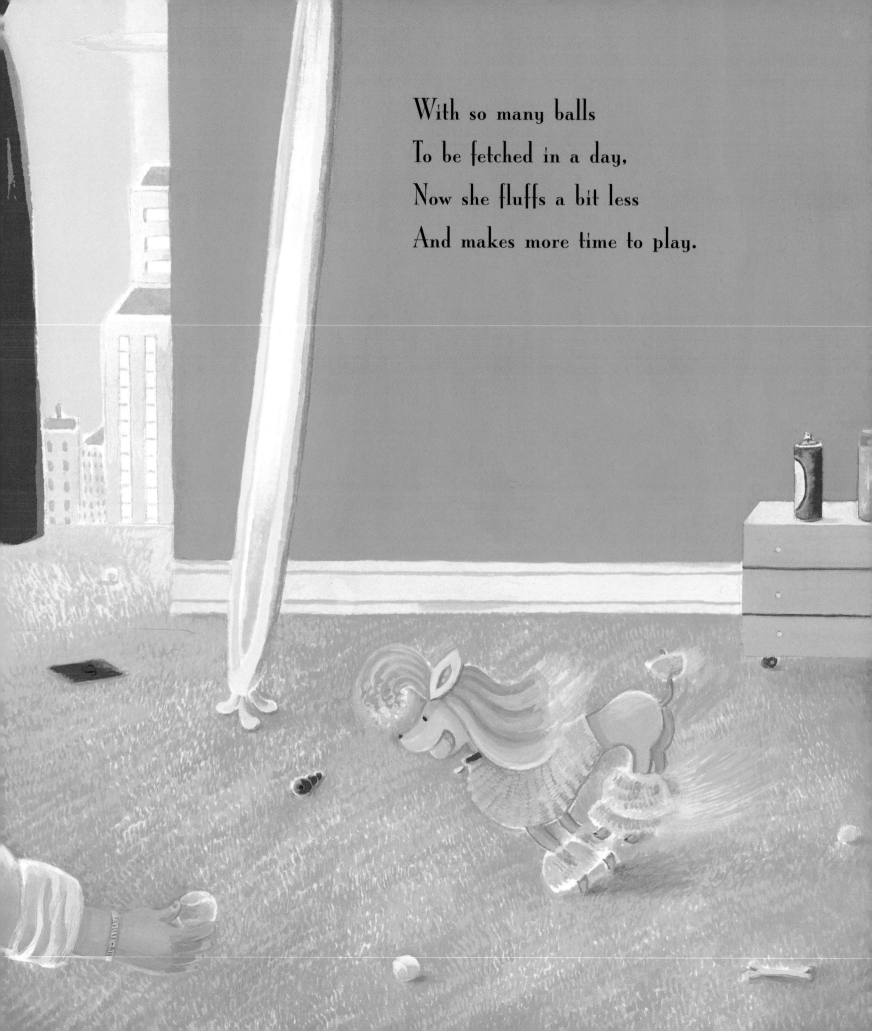

One powder with pink
And then off to the park...

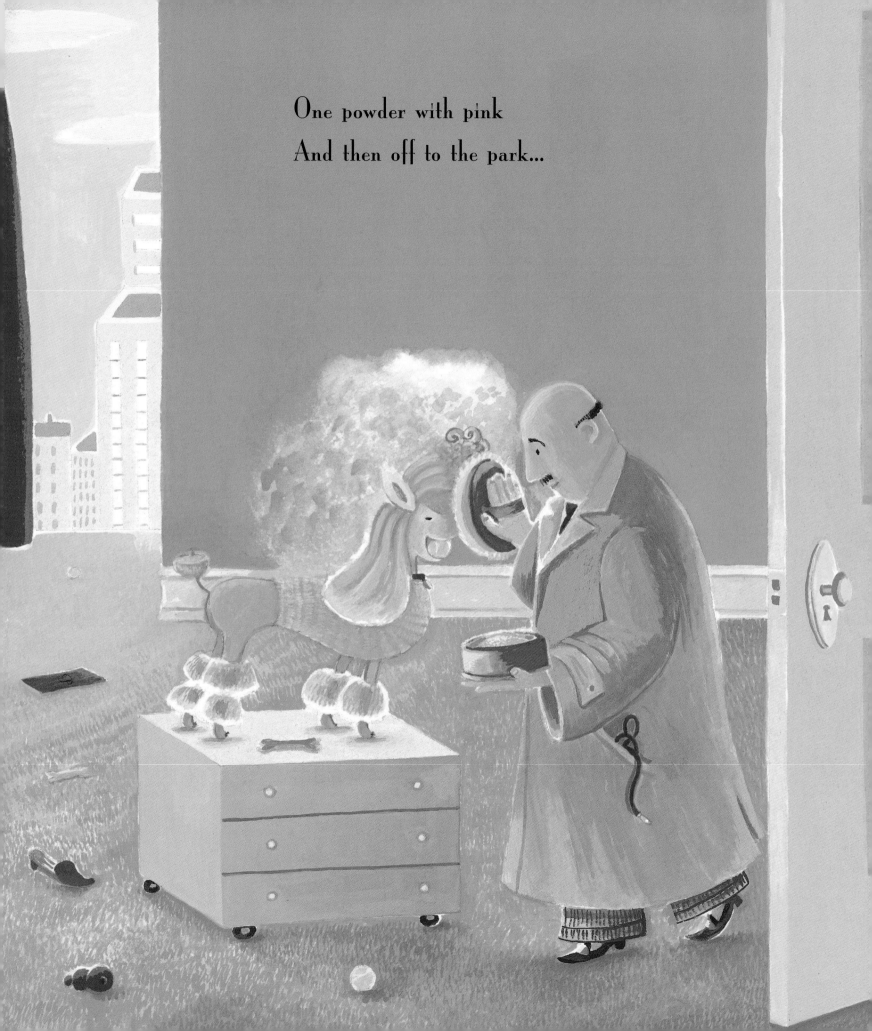

To chase balls on the green
And get dirty till dark.